WHO'S YOUR DADDY?

WHO'S YOUR DADDY?

I Know Mine, Do You?

Reggie J. Polite

XULON PRESS

Xulon Press
2301 Lucien Way #415
Maitland, FL 32751
407.339.4217
www.xulonpress.com

© 2020 by Reggie J. Polite

All rights reserved solely by the author. The author guarantees all contents are original and do not infringe upon the legal rights of any other person or work. No part of this book may be reproduced in any form without the permission of the author. The views expressed in this book are not necessarily those of the publisher.

Unless otherwise indicated, Scripture quotations taken from the Holy Bible, New International Version (NIV). Copyright © 1973, 1978, 1984, 2011 by Biblica, Inc.™. Used by permission. All rights reserved.

Printed in the United States of America.

ISBN-13: 978-1-6305-0725-1

Introduction

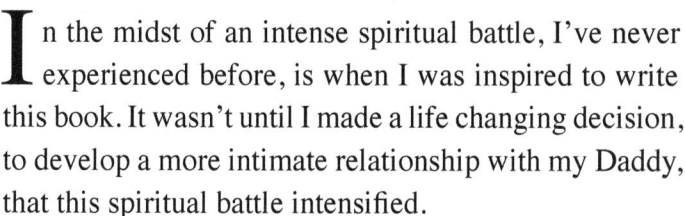

In the midst of an intense spiritual battle, I've never experienced before, is when I was inspired to write this book. It wasn't until I made a life changing decision, to develop a more intimate relationship with my Daddy, that this spiritual battle intensified.

We all have or had a father. His love for you may not have been what you wanted or expected it to be; or, maybe, it was just everything you wanted and/or expected it to be. We all have different experiences. But, regardless, whatever the experience was or continues to be to this day, he is limited in all that he wants to do for you and in all he can do for you. Why is that? Because he is no different than you. He experiences the same challenges you do. But not my Daddy.

Who's Your Daddy?

This book is about my Daddy. It's about who He is and who He isn't. Many think they know Him and many do not. I want you to get to know Him for yourself, because that's what He wants. He wants a personal relationship with you. My Daddy is not mysterious or secretive. There's nothing strange about him. He's not unpleasant to be around nor is He hostile by nature. Get to know Him for yourself.

Where are You?
I was walking in the cool of the day,
To fellowship with my friend.
To show him my Way.
Where are You?
You used to run to me, arms opened wide,
to hug me,
But you are nowhere to be found.
Where are You?
Hidden and ashamed – you ran away,
Only to point the blame.
Don't you know my Love for You, will never fade?
Where are You?[1]

---

[1] Author

Introduction

Who's your Daddy? Do you really know? Is he a present help in the time of trouble; in the time of distress and misfortune? What's so special about him? What makes him different? Is he always honest with you? Is he always there for you no matter what? Does he really love you, unconditionally? Are you truly his beloved? Who's your Daddy?

Before I begin to share with you who my Daddy is, let me first share with you how I've come to really know of Him. It all started with my mom. She never forced-fed Him on me or my siblings, but she always spoke of Him. Every opportunity she had, she'd always talk to us about Him. She would always mention how good he was to her and to us. Even up until the time she was no longer able, as a result of her descending physical condition, to open her mouth to express her love for Him. I know her love for Daddy never ceased.

I heard others talk about Daddy; relatives, friends, etc.; especially, from those, of course, who professed, and continue to profess, to know Him. And they all had, and continue to have, their own opinions about Daddy. But for many of them, they saw, and continue to see Him as a: *burden, demanding, difficult, manipulating, mysterious*, *old*, and a *phony – imaginary*. That's because they just only know of Him.

Many didn't like Him and many were afraid of Him. Many didn't care for Him or just didn't know what to make of Him – just really didn't know Him. The latter was even true for me at one time, to be honest. But when I decided to really get to know Him, by spending quality time with Him, that's when I really got to know who He is and who He is not.

I remember clearly Him saying to me, back in 1993, these words: *"Many people think they know me, but they don't."* Although my mom would periodically talk to us about Daddy, me personally, I didn't know Him as Daddy. I just knew of Him.

Unfortunately, to know Him personally as Daddy, ignorantly and/or traditionally, we left up to others who "supposedly" knew or know Him, to tell us about Him. There were those who sincerely spoke of Daddy because of their unadulterated personal relationship they had with Him. Others, however, spoke of Him out of duty, for selfish reasons, for personal gain, or just out of plain ignorance. They didn't really know Him; they only knew of Him. This is still true even today for many. They really don't know Daddy.

Introduction

To them who really know Him personally, which may be people you may already know, who really "hang-out" with Him consistently and qualitatively to this day, spoke of and continue to speak of His *affection*, His *compassion* and His *generosity*.

So, let me begin by telling you who my Daddy is not.

Who My Daddy Is Not!

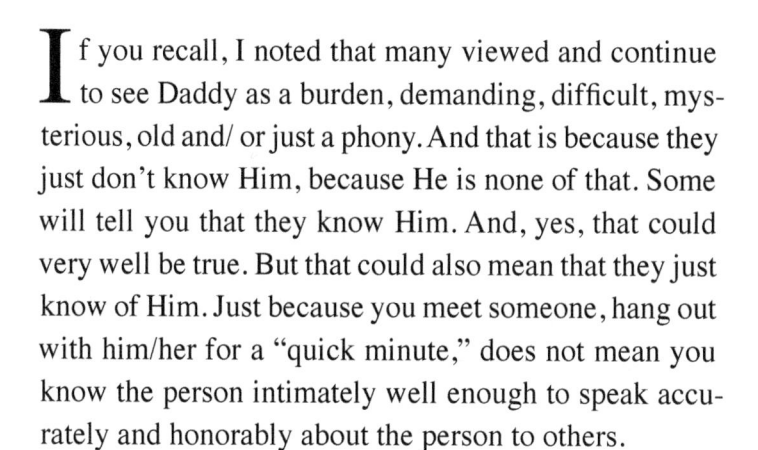

If you recall, I noted that many viewed and continue to see Daddy as a burden, demanding, difficult, mysterious, old and/ or just a phony. And that is because they just don't know Him, because He is none of that. Some will tell you that they know Him. And, yes, that could very well be true. But that could also mean that they just know of Him. Just because you meet someone, hang out with him/her for a "quick minute," does not mean you know the person intimately well enough to speak accurately and honorably about the person to others.

Ask yourself: Would you want a person who does not know you, who doesn't spend quality time with you on a daily basis, to represent you and to speak formally about you to others? Wouldn't you prefer for whosoever wants to get to know the real you, that they spend consistent quality time with you so that they will know who you are for themselves? I know I would.

If anyone spoke ill words about someone, which we have a personal relationship with, we normally would respond by saying something like: *"That's not so-and-so"*; *"I don't know him/her like that"*; *"You're wrong"*; *"You don't know what you are talking about"*; *"You really need to get to know him/her"* and/or, *"That's not true about him/her"*. That's just some of the things we'd say in defense of someone we have a relationship with – someone we know. Bottom line, we'd speak up on their behalf to defend their character.

Well, Daddy is not a burden to anyone. He is not about deliberately causing anyone problems, nor is He about causing stress in your life. That's not who He is. You're wrong if you think of Him in that way; neither is He about wanting to cause affliction or vexation. That's not His M.O.

I don't know Him as one who'd aggressively pressure or intimidate anyone to get what He wants, as that's not Daddy. He is not about tormenting you. He's not shrewd or calculating, as we sometimes can behave. That's just not in Him. Who told you all this? You just don't know what you are talking about if you believe

Who My Daddy Is Not!

that about my Daddy. You just know of Him from what you've heard. You really need to get to know Him, personally, for yourself.

Daddy is not demanding. He is not looking for you to perform pious acts to please Him or to meet burdensome expectations. He is not depending on you, nor is he looking for you to provide for Him. That's not true about Him. You're mistaken to say or think that about Him.

He is not about criticizing you for your failures, nor is He a fault-finder, as we have the tendency to be toward each other and toward ourselves. One thing for sure, Daddy is definitely not a grouch. You are wrong to believe and say that about Him. He's not against you! He is for you! He'll never think of you or see you as a loser. Why would you believe or think that of Him? Why would you believe that about my Daddy? Maybe it is because you only just know of Him.

My Daddy is not difficult, because He is not into causing you hardships or problems. He doesn't go out of his way to make it hard for you or anyone, just to please Himself. His ways are nowhere like ours, as that's not Daddy. He won't treat you inappropriately. Is that what you heard? You heard incorrectly if you think of Him in that way, so get to know Him for yourself.

Who's Your Daddy?

He is not about being tough with you. Who told you that? He's not violent nor is He unruly. He's not about being threatening or unforgiving in His relationships with anyone. Where did you get that? You don't know what you are talking about if you believe that is my Daddy. You really need to get to know Him, personally, for yourself.

Daddy is not mysterious or secretive. There's nothing strange about him. He is not difficult or impossible to understand, and there's nothing even dark about Him. His way of thinking is just more advanced. His disposition is not of someone who is shady. He's not unpleasant to be around, nor is He hostile by nature. Where did you get that from? Daddy is not about withholding His perspectives, plans, or thoughts with His family or friends. That's not who He is. You don't know what you are talking about if you believe those things to be true about my Daddy. You don't know Him.

My Daddy is not old. He is not broken-down or "over-the-hill." He's not immobile nor is He a "stiff" or a statue; not my Daddy. If you believe that about Him, you really don't know Him. He's not even senile or blind. You're wrong if you accuse or think of Him in that way. My Daddy is not forgetful. For sure, He is not lazy. You don't know what you are talking about if you believe any of this about my Daddy.

Daddy is not a phony, a fraud or a fake. You're mistaken to say or think that about Him. He is not some con-artist, a cheat, or about trickery. That's not my Daddy, as He is not into practicing deception. He is not dishonest and He is not an illusionist. Believe that about my Daddy. Get to know Him, personally, for yourself.

Those are only some of the views many people use to describe Daddy. There are many more inaccurate opinions to describe his character, but just let me say this: He is ***transparent***, ***comprehensive,*** and ***unique***–not your "typical" dad.

He will not curse you! He is nowhere near like any of the people you've come into contact with and know. And once you develop a relationship with Him, then you'll get to really know Him for yourself. I will say, however, that He highly detests these individual acts of behaviors: *walking in conceit*; *concocting immoral plots*; *hasty to participate in mischief*; *being two-faced*; *committed to injurious testimony*; *provokes dissonance;* and *performing unlawful and premeditated shedding of innocent blood*. He shares no part in those sorts of behaviors.

Who's Your Daddy?

Now, let me tell you who Daddy is. But first, let me be very clear: He adopted me into His very large family, as that was His plan for me on day one! And when you meet my Dad for YOURSELF and desire to intimately get to know Him, you'll also want to be adopted into His family, because then you'll know Him just as I do.

Who My Daddy Is?

My Daddy is *affectionate*, *compassionate* and *generous*. But He is even more than that! For you to know the "even more" about Daddy, you'll need to spend quality time with Him. Just you and Him; not just for a day, but for every day of your life. In fact, my Daddy is always available. He wants a relationship with you, so just come as you are. He wants you to know Him for yourself. He is big on that. He is always open to have a discussion with you. And He'd be honest with you. He doesn't think the way we do, nor does He approach circumstances or situations like we do. Like I said, Daddy is not common.

Daddy has a very big heart, and very tender-hearted. He speaks softly and His words are comforting. That is Daddy! True to His word, you can rely on what He says to you. Daddy is committed to wanting a relationship with anyone. That's who He is, and His affection is immeasurable. I know what I am talking about. You should want to get to know Daddy.

Daddy really cares about you. I am not wrong when I say or think that about Him. He is concerned about your well-being. That's Daddy! Daddy has feelings for you. He hurts with you. He understands you. My Daddy wants to hold you in His arms, and wants you to feel His awesome touch. That's who He is. I know what I am talking about. Get to know Him for yourself.

Daddy is always ready to help meet your needs, for that's what I know about Him. He goes "above and beyond" what you ask of Him. He's awesome! You should want to get to know Him, as He won't turn you or anyone away. There is no limit to Daddy's generosity, because it is inexhaustible. That's who He is. I know what I am talking about.

He is more than all that! All of what I just shared with you describing my Daddy is minuscule compared to ALL that He is. There is a lot more to Him! Just hearing about Him is not enough; likewise, just knowing of Him is not enough. It's a good start, but you need to spend time with Him; quality time for yourself, to experience all that He is and to intimately know who He is. What you may be hearing could be inaccurate or untrue, or both.

I say this from experience; I've been there. What I heard about Him, I believed. I was fearful of Him and afraid to make a mistake. But guess what? I made a whole bunch of them. And, also, guess what? I am here telling you; He is not someone to be fearful of.

What you're hearing from others may have some truth about Him in it, but it may not be the complete characterization of who He is. He definitely doesn't want your relationship with Him to be shallow or to make you feel like you're in bondage.

He is more than just "a man." Once you are convinced of that, I am certain you'll want to call Him your Father for yourself. Oh, and the benefits of accepting adoption into His family and maintaining an intimate relationship with Him are real, unchangeable and life changing. But you will never experience it all, apart from His family.

Family Benefits

"If it sounds too good to be true, it ain't." Let me tell you, NEVER with Daddy!

1. **<u>FAMILY</u>:** Once YOU make the decision to be part of Daddy's family, there is only acceptance! Accepted no matter what you look like or don't look like. Whether you call yourself illegitimate or not. It doesn't matter what you did or didn't accomplish in life. Regardless of your past failures, mistakes, decisions, actions, whatever; YOU are ACCEPTED with OPEN ARMS. That's because of Daddy's love. No rejection. It's unconditional and unwavering. No expiration, as that is who He is.

Who's Your Daddy?

You have free and direct access to Him all the time, anytime. It's awesome! You are never alone in His family. There's a relationship. The closer you get to Daddy, the closer He gets to you. That's what He wants, a relationship with you.

2. **HEIR:** You are a joint heir. Yep, everything that Daddy owns belongs to you. Ask Him and He will answer. No favorites. All that He has is available to you. Let me be clear: This inheritance doesn't decay or diminish. If you don't believe me, learn it for yourself. He withholds nothing from His family. You are considered no less or greater than the other family members. He doesn't care about your background from which you come. No one is better than the other, regardless. All in Daddy's family are equals!

3. **PROVISION:** In a dire situation? In a crisis? Go right to Him. Better yet, RUN toward Him! In fact, He'll RUN to you with open arms. Even if you are at fault, go to Him. Daddy is not going to hold anything against you. That's not how He

Family Benefits

operates with His family. Daddy got your back and so does His family.

There is stability. Everything you will ever need is provided, whatever it is. It's there for the taking. You never have to worry about Him running out of what you need. Are you weary with life? His arms are open wide, waiting for YOU.

Daddy's got your back. Daddy will ALWAYS meet you at your point of need. Anytime! Anywhere! Any day! Taste and see for yourself.

4. **IDENTITY:** With Daddy, there is no identity crisis. In His family, you take on His name. As you maintain and grow your relationship with Him, your countenance will commence to change. You will start looking like Daddy. You won't see the change. Others will see the outward change, which started inwardly.

You inherit Daddy's name, Living Stone, and His persona. You'll begin to take on a new attitude toward life and others. You'll know who you really are, not what others have said or what you once believed about you.

Your confidence will begin to build. You'll learn to become more alert and clear-headed, which is because of your assurance in the relationship you have with Daddy.

5. **PEACE:** We all experience grief and challenges in our lives. It comes with living on this earth. As you grow and maintain your relationship with Daddy, no matter what challenges you face—oh yeah, you will have life challenges coming at you like never before once you join His family—you will experience an unexplainable, incomprehensible peace in the midst of chaos. Not the two-finger peace sign either.

In addition, Daddy has a way to make your "enemies" become at peace with you. Now, I didn't say that they will like you. They'll just be at peace with you, which they won't be able to explain why. It will just happen.

These are just some of His benefits. There are so much more that they are life changing!

So, again, I ask.

Who's your Daddy? Do you really know? Is He a present help in the time of trouble? What's so special about Him? What makes Him different? Is He always

Family Benefits

honest with you? Is He always there for you no matter what? Is He a present support in the time of distress and misfortune? Does He really love you, regardless? Are you truly His beloved? I can answer yes to all those questions because I made a decision to be accepted into His family and you can also.

To get to know Him for yourself the way He wants you to, this is what Daddy said: *"This is my Son, whom I love; with him I am well pleased. Listen to Him!" (Matt. 17:5[b]). He* is speaking of JESUS. You have to accept His son Jesus, who makes it very clear: *"I am the way and the truth and the life. No one comes to the Father except through me" (John 14:6).*

> **See the animal in the cages,**
> **Can't go where they want to be.**
> **I wonder why I get this feeling,**
> **The one who was really caged, was me.**
> **Slavery, where's the Key, where's the Door?**
> **I was reading somewhere in some pages,**
> **About a man from Galilee.**
> **Could the things that they were saying,**
> **Could this Man love someone like me?**
> **When the Son sets you free,**

Who's Your Daddy?

**You're free indeed,
And only HE is the one,
that set me free,
from the chains which were binding me.
He helped me understand,
how I fit into His plan.
Because He is the only one who can help me.[2]**

"If God were your Father, you would love me, for I have come here from God. I have not come on my own, God sent me." (John 8:42)

What's indubitably true: Jesus walked this earth as a "son of man" and died for YOUR sins--the sin you were born into and the sin you had nothing to do with--to reconcile you to Daddy. The love He has for you was not without pain. It's not superficial, candy, flowers, jewelry etc., it's more than that! It's impactful! All of Daddy's love may bring about some discomfort, but it is worth it! It's life–changing!

To reject Jesus, you reject Daddy and His love. It's a choice. Daddy is a gentleman. He will never force you to do anything.

---

[2] Author

Family Benefits

In the morning,
I will sing of your great strength.
In the morning,
I will sing of your great love.
For you are my fortress/My refuge/in times
of trouble,
You are my strength/I will sing praise to you.
Abba/Father in the morning,
Abba/Father in the noon day.
My Daddy/All Day, Every day!
In the morning.[3]

---

[3] Author

CPSIA information can be obtained
at www.ICGtesting.com
Printed in the USA
LVHW050352200221
679374LV00008B/446